THE LI

OF

PAUL O'GRADY

The Biography of a Legend: A captivating journey of resilience, Laughter and Philanthropy

Dave Watson

Public

The Life Paul O'Grady

ISBN: 9798398602128

Cover illustration and content by Dave Watson

For permissions or inquiries, please contact djb20182018@gmail.com

Table of Contents:

Introduction

Paul O'Grady is a name that has become synonymous with wit, charisma, and an indomitable spirit. From humble beginnings to becoming a household name, O'Grady's life has been a remarkable journey of triumphs, challenges, and a relentless pursuit of his dreams. In this book, we delve into the captivating life of Paul O'Grady, exploring the man behind the persona, his rise to stardom, his philanthropy, and the lasting impact he has made on the entertainment industry.

Chapter 1 sets the stage, providing an overview of the purpose of this book and offering readers a glimpse into the extraordinary life of Paul O'Grady. Born in a working-class family, O'Grady's childhood was shaped by a mixture of love, laughter, and the challenges of everyday life. It was during these formative years that his passion for performance and entertainment began to take root.

In Chapter 2, we explore O'Grady's childhood and early influences. Growing up in the vibrant city of Liverpool, he was surrounded by a rich cultural tapestry that would shape his comedic sensibilities and love for the arts. We delve into the impact of his family background, the supportive relationships he formed, and the experiences that ignited his creativity and set him on a path toward a career in show business.

The journey toward stardom forms the heart of Chapter 3. We trace O'Grady's early steps in the entertainment industry, from local gigs to the pivotal moments that propelled him into the limelight. It was his unique blend of humor, quick wit, and magnetic stage presence that captivated audiences and opened doors to numerous opportunities. However, this chapter also sheds light on the challenges and setbacks O'Grady faced along the way, reminding us that success rarely comes without its fair share of obstacles.

Chapter 4 delves into the birth of Lily Savage, the iconic drag queen persona that became synonymous with Paul O'Grady. We uncover the creative process behind the character's development, exploring the inspirations, influences, and transformative power of Lily Savage. From underground cabaret clubs to nationwide fame, we witness the ascent of this larger-than-life persona and the impact it had on O'Grady's career.

Television became a significant platform for O'Grady's talent, and Chapter 5 explores his various TV shows and appearances. From hosting his own talk shows to unforgettable collaborations with fellow entertainers, O'Grady's versatility, and ability to connect with audiences were evident throughout his television career. This chapter also shines a light on his exploration of other creative avenues beyond the small screen.

While O'Grady's success in the entertainment industry is undeniable, Chapter 6 delves into his philanthropy and activism. Behind the laughter and glitter, O'Grady has consistently used his platform to champion charitable causes, supporting those in need and lending his voice to campaigns that make a difference. We examine the depth of his involvement in philanthropy and the impact his efforts have had on society.

Chapter 7 offers a glimpse into O'Grady's personal life and relationships, shedding light on the man behind the public persona. Balancing fame and personal life is no easy feat, and this chapter explores the joys, challenges, and milestones that have shaped O'Grady's personal journey.

The subsequent chapter, Chapter 8, delves into the challenges and triumphs that have defined O'Grady's life. From personal struggles to professional hurdles, he has faced adversity head-on, emerging stronger and more resilient. We explore the pivotal moments that tested his mettle, the lessons learned along the way, and the growth he experienced as an individual.

In Chapter 9, we reflect on O'Grady's legacy and influence. His contributions to the entertainment industry have left an indelible mark, inspiring future generations of performers and pushing the boundaries of comedy and entertainment. We examine his cultural significance, highlighting the enduring impact he has made and the ways in which he will continue to shape the industry for years to come.

As we conclude this book in Chapter 10, we reflect on the extraordinary life of Paul O'Grady. We explore the depth of his talent, the challenges he overcame, and the indomitable spirit that propelled him forward. His journey serves as an inspiration to all, reminding us that with passion, perseverance, and a dash of humor, we can overcome any obstacle and leave a lasting legacy.

In "The Life of Paul O'Grady," we embark on a captivating exploration of a man who defied the odds, brought laughter to millions, and used his platform for the betterment of society. Through the pages of this book, we invite you to join us on a remarkable journey, celebrating the life and achievements of a true entertainment legend.

CHAPTER ONE

1.1 The purpose of the book

The purpose of the book "The Life of Paul O'Grady" is to provide readers with an in-depth and captivating account of the extraordinary life and career of Paul O'Grady. This book aims to celebrate his achievements, shed light on his journey from humble beginnings to becoming a beloved and influential figure in the entertainment industry, and explore the impact he has made on both the cultural landscape and the lives of individuals.

By delving into the personal and professional experiences of Paul O'Grady, this book seeks to inspire and entertain readers. It aims to showcase the resilience, determination, and talent that propelled O'Grady to success, highlighting the challenges he faced and the triumphs he achieved along the way. Through his story, readers can find inspiration in pursuing their passions, overcoming obstacles, and leaving a meaningful impact on the world.

Furthermore, "The Life of Paul O'Grady" aims to honor O'Grady's contributions to philanthropy and activism. By exploring his involvement in charitable causes and advocacy work, the book seeks to inspire readers to consider the power of using their platform and resources to create positive change in society.

Above all, this book serves as a tribute to the life, career, and legacy of Paul O'Grady. It aims to engage and captivate readers, offering a deeper understanding of the man behind the persona, his journey to stardom, and the lasting influence he has had on the entertainment industry and beyond.

1.2 A brief overview of Paul O'Grady's Life and Achievements

Paul O'Grady is a renowned British entertainer and television personality who has captivated audiences with his wit, charm, and versatile talent. Born on June 14, 1955, in Birkenhead, England, O'Grady's journey from modest beginnings to becoming a household name is nothing short of remarkable.

In his early years, O'Grady's passion for performance and entertainment began to take shape. Growing up in Liverpool, a city known for its vibrant cultural scene, he was exposed to a rich tapestry of music, comedy, and theater. These influences ignited his creativity and set him on a path toward a career in show business.

O'Grady's breakthrough came in the form of his alter ego, Lily Savage. Lily, a larger-than-life drag queen persona, became a sensation both on the cabaret circuit and in mainstream entertainment. With her sharp tongue, quick wit, and fabulous attire, Lily Savage quickly gained a devoted following and propelled O'Grady into the national spotlight.

Television became a significant platform for O'Grady's talent, and he hosted several successful shows, including "The Paul O'Grady Show" and "Paul O'Grady Live." Known for his effortless ability to connect with guests and audiences alike, O'Grady's shows were a blend of engaging interviews, hilarious sketches, and memorable musical performances.

Beyond his television work, O'Grady has also made notable contributions to the theater world. He has appeared in various stage productions, including the West End musical "Priscilla, Queen of the Desert," where he showcased his flair for performance and delighted audiences with his comedic timing.

While O'Grady's accomplishments in the entertainment industry are impressive, his influence extends far beyond the stage and screen. He has been actively involved in philanthropy and has used his platform to raise awareness and support for numerous charitable causes. O'Grady's advocacy work has included campaigns for animal welfare, LGBTQ+ rights, and various healthcare initiatives.

In recognition of his contributions to the entertainment industry and his philanthropic efforts, O'Grady has received numerous accolades and honors throughout his career. These include several National Television Awards, a BAFTA Special Award, and an MBE (Member of the Order of the British Empire) for his services to entertainment.

Paul O'Grady's life and achievements serve as a testament to the power of talent, perseverance, and a genuine connection with audiences. From his humble beginnings in Liverpool to becoming a beloved figure in British entertainment, O'Grady's journey is a source of inspiration and a testament to the lasting impact one person can have on the world through their art and advocacy.

CHAPTER TWO

2. Childhood and Early Influences

Paul O'Grady's childhood and early influences played a pivotal role in shaping his love for performance and setting the foundation for his future success in the entertainment industry.

Born on June 14, 1955, in Birkenhead, England, O'Grady grew up in a working-class family. He was the youngest of five children, and his childhood was filled with the love, laughter, and occasional hardships that come with such an environment. His parents, Patrick, and Mary O'Grady, instilled in him a strong work ethic and a sense of humor that would later become trademarks of his career.

Growing up in Liverpool, O'Grady was surrounded by a vibrant cultural scene. The city's music, comedy, and theatrical offerings provided a rich tapestry for his young mind to explore. From an early age, O'Grady showed a keen interest in entertainment, often immersing himself in the local theater scene and soaking up the performances that unfolded before his eyes.

In his formative years, O'Grady was exposed to a variety of influences that would shape his comedic sensibilities and ignite his passion for performance. He was particularly drawn to the sharp wit and irreverent humor of comedians such as Ken Dodd and Tommy Cooper, who left a lasting impression on his comedic style.

Additionally, O'Grady found inspiration in the music and artistry of Liverpool's iconic band, The Beatles. Their groundbreaking music and innovative approach to creativity resonated with him, showcasing the transformative power of artistic expression and influencing his own aspirations.

During his youth, O'Grady also developed a fascination with drag queens, an interest that would later manifest in his iconic persona, Lily

Savage. He was captivated by their larger-than-life personalities, glamorous costumes, and the way they commanded attention and adoration on stage. This early exposure to the world of drag would plant the seeds for his future transformation into Lily Savage, an alter ego that would bring him national fame and acclaim.

While O'Grady's childhood was filled with influences that ignited his passion for performance, it wasn't without its challenges. Coming from a working-class background, he faced the societal expectations and limitations that often accompany such circumstances. However, his love for entertainment and his natural talent provided an escape from those constraints, allowing him to pursue his dreams against the odds.

Paul O'Grady's childhood and early influences served as a catalyst for his journey into the entertainment industry. The love and laughter he experienced at home, coupled with the vibrant cultural scene of Liverpool, nurtured his comedic sensibilities and kindled his desire to make people laugh. It was during these formative years that O'Grady discovered his calling, setting him on a path that would ultimately lead to his remarkable success as an entertainer.

2.1 Family Background and Upbringing

Paul O'Grady's family background and upbringing played a significant role in shaping the person he would become and influencing his journey into the entertainment industry.

O'Grady was born into a working-class family on June 14, 1955, in Birkenhead, England. His parents, Patrick, and Mary O'Grady, provided a loving and supportive environment for him and his four siblings. Growing up, O'Grady experienced the typical joys and challenges that come with being part of a close-knit family.

His father, Patrick, worked as a docker, while his mother, Mary, took on various jobs to support the family. They instilled in their children a strong work ethic and the importance of perseverance. The values of hard work, determination, and resilience would become guiding principles in O'Grady's own life and career.

Despite their modest means, O'Grady's parents encouraged his interests and nurtured his creative spirit. They recognized his love for performance from an early age and supported his dreams of pursuing a career in entertainment. Their belief in him helped foster his self-confidence and provided the foundation for his future success.

O'Grady's upbringing was filled with the warmth, laughter, and occasional hardships that often accompany a working-class household. The close bond he shared with his siblings and the shared experiences of navigating life's challenges together forged a strong sense of family unity that would remain with him throughout his life.

In his later years, O'Grady spoke fondly of the humor and wit that permeated his childhood home. The O'Grady household was often filled with laughter and banter, with family members engaging in lively conversations and exchanges. This environment not only nurtured O'Grady's own sense of humor but also provided the inspiration for the comedic timing and sharp wit that would later become hallmarks of his career.

As O'Grady embarked on his journey into the entertainment industry, his family's support remained unwavering. Their encouragement and belief in his talent fueled his determination to succeed, even in the face of challenges and setbacks.

The values and experiences instilled in O'Grady by his family would shape his character and influence his approach to his work and personal life. The love, resilience, and humor he learned from his parents and siblings would become integral aspects of his personality and would shine through in his performances and interactions with others.

Paul O'Grady's family background and upbringing provided a solid foundation for his journey into the entertainment industry. The support, love, and values instilled by his working-class family played a vital role in shaping the person he became—an entertainer who captivated audiences with his talent, wit, and authenticity.

2.2 Early interests and passions

During his early years, Paul O'Grady developed a range of interests and passions that would later shape his career in the entertainment industry. From a young age, it was evident that O'Grady had a natural inclination for performance and a deep love for the arts.

One of his earliest passions was music. Growing up in Liverpool, a city known for its rich musical heritage, O'Grady was exposed to a wide variety of music genres and artists. He developed a deep appreciation for music and its ability to evoke emotions and connect people. This love for music would later influence his career, as he incorporated music into his performances and even embarked on ventures as a singer.

Comedy also held a special place in O'Grady's heart. He was drawn to the power of laughter and the way comedians could captivate audiences with their wit and humor. O'Grady's comedic sensibilities were influenced by comedians such as Ken Dodd and Tommy Cooper, whose performances left a lasting impression on him. Their ability to entertain and make people laugh would serve as inspiration for his own comedic style.

Additionally, O'Grady had a fascination with the world of drag queens. He was captivated by their extravagant costumes, larger-than-life personas, and the way they commanded attention on stage. This early interest would later manifest in the creation of his iconic drag queen persona, Lily Savage. Lily became an integral part of O'Grady's career, allowing him to express his creativity, showcase his comedic talents, and connect with audiences in a unique and memorable way.

The theater scene in Liverpool also captured O'Grady's imagination. He immersed himself in the local theater community, attending performances and becoming captivated by the magic of live theater. This exposure to the world of theater nurtured his love for storytelling, character development, and the transformative power of the stage.

Furthermore, O'Grady had a natural affinity for storytelling. From a young age, he possessed a vivid imagination and a knack for spinning tales that captivated those around him. This storytelling ability would later be honed and showcased in his television shows, where he would engage audiences with humorous anecdotes and captivating narratives.

Overall, O'Grady's early interests and passions set the stage for his career in the entertainment industry. His love for music, comedy, drag, theater, and storytelling would converge to form the foundation of his multifaceted talent and contribute to the unique charm that endeared him to audiences. These early passions would fuel his journey, propelling him forward as he pursued his dreams and left an indelible mark on the world of entertainment.

2.3 Key Experiences and Influences

Paul O'Grady's life has been shaped by various key experiences and influences that have had a significant impact on his career and personal development. These experiences and influences have contributed to shaping his unique persona, his comedic style, and his perspective on life.

1. The City of Liverpool: O'Grady's upbringing in Liverpool, a city known for its vibrant cultural scene, had a profound influence on him. The city's rich musical heritage, theater productions, and comedic traditions provided a fertile ground for O'Grady to explore and develop his own talents. The artistic atmosphere of Liverpool instilled in him a sense of creativity and nurtured his passion for performance.

2. The Drag Queen Scene: O'Grady's fascination with drag queens played a pivotal role in his career. He was captivated by their larger-than-life personalities, flamboyant costumes, and the way they commanded attention on stage. This early interest in drag queens paved the way for his iconic drag persona, Lily Savage. The drag queen scene influenced his comedic style, giving him the freedom to push boundaries, challenge norms, and captivate audiences with his quick wit and biting humor.

3. Personal Challenges and Resilience: O'Grady faced personal challenges throughout his life, including periods of illness and personal loss. These experiences tested his resilience and shaped his outlook on life. O'Grady's ability to find humor even in difficult situations became a defining characteristic of his comedic style. He channeled his personal struggles into his performances, using laughter as a means of healing and connecting with audiences on a deeper level.

4. Television Success: O'Grady's breakthrough in television, particularly with shows like "The Paul O'Grady Show" and "Paul O'Grady Live," propelled him to national fame and acclaim. His ability to connect with guests and audiences, his quick wit, and his genuine warmth endeared him to viewers across the country. These experiences in television solidified his position as a beloved and respected figure in the entertainment industry.

5. Philanthropy and Activism: O'Grady's commitment to philanthropy and activism has been a significant influence on his life. He has used his platform to raise awareness and support for various charitable causes, particularly those related to animal welfare, LGBTQ+ rights, and healthcare initiatives. O'Grady's advocacy work reflects his compassionate nature and his desire to make a positive impact on society beyond his entertainment career.

6. Personal Relationships: The relationships O'Grady has cultivated throughout his life have also played a crucial role in shaping him.

Whether it be his close bonds with family members, cherished friendships, or romantic partnerships, these relationships have provided support, love, and inspiration. The connections he has formed with loved ones have influenced his outlook on life, fueled his creativity, and provided a strong foundation of support throughout his journey.

These key experiences and influences have shaped Paul O'Grady's career, molded his comedic style, and contributed to his enduring popularity. From the vibrant city of Liverpool to personal triumphs and challenges, these factors have shaped his unique perspective, allowing him to touch the lives of millions with his talent, humor, and compassionate spirit.

CHAPTER THREE

3. The Path to Stardom

Paul O'Grady's path to stardom is a testament to his talent, perseverance, and ability to connect with audiences. His journey from humble beginnings to becoming a household name in the entertainment industry is a remarkable story of hard work and determination.

O'Grady's first steps towards stardom can be traced back to his early years in Liverpool. Immersed in the city's vibrant cultural scene, he honed his comedic skills and developed a passion for performance. Inspired by the humor of comedians like Ken Dodd and Tommy Cooper, O'Grady began to cultivate his own comedic style, characterized by sharp wit and irreverent humor.

His breakthrough came in the form of his drag queen persona, Lily Savage. With her larger-than-life personality, glamorous attire, and quick tongue, Lily Savage captured the attention of audiences and catapulted O'Grady into the national spotlight. His performances as Lily Savage on the cabaret circuit garnered a devoted following and established him as a rising star in the entertainment industry.

Television became a significant platform for O'Grady's talent. He hosted a series of successful shows, including "The Paul O'Grady Show" and "Paul O'Grady Live," where he showcased his versatility as an entertainer. With his infectious charm, genuine warmth, and ability to connect with guests and viewers, O'Grady endeared himself to a wide audience, becoming a beloved figure in British television.

Beyond his television work, O'Grady ventured into other areas of entertainment. He demonstrated his vocal prowess by releasing music albums, showcasing his singing abilities. O'Grady also made notable contributions to the theater world, appearing in various stage productions and earning critical acclaim for his performances.

and the genuine connection he forges with those who have had the pleasure of experiencing his performances.

3.3 Challenges and setbacks faced along the way.

Paul O'Grady's journey to success has not been without its share of challenges and setbacks. Throughout his career, he has faced various obstacles that tested his resilience, determination, and ability to overcome adversity. These challenges have shaped him as an individual and added depth to his remarkable story of triumph.

1. Personal Loss: O'Grady has experienced significant personal loss throughout his life. The untimely deaths of his mother and close friends deeply impacted him, leaving a void that was difficult to fill. These losses took a toll on his emotional well-being and required him to navigate through grief while maintaining his professional commitments. O'Grady's ability to find strength in the face of such personal tragedy is a testament to his resilience.

2. Health Struggles: O'Grady has faced health challenges that have impacted his career. In 2001, he suffered a heart attack, which forced him to reassess his lifestyle and prioritize his well-being. O'Grady's determination to regain his health and continue pursuing his passion in the entertainment industry is a testament to his resilience and determination.

3. Professional Setbacks: Like many entertainers, O'Grady has experienced professional setbacks throughout his career. These setbacks could range from show cancellations to projects that didn't achieve the desired success. However, O'Grady's ability to adapt, evolve, and continue pursuing new opportunities demonstrates his tenacity and commitment to his craft.

4. Public Scrutiny: As a prominent figure in the public eye, O'Grady has faced scrutiny and criticism. The pressures of fame and public

expectations can be overwhelming, impacting one's personal and professional life. O'Grady has weathered such scrutiny with grace, maintaining his authenticity and staying true to himself despite external pressures.

5. Balancing Personal and Professional Life: The demanding nature of a career in the entertainment industry often presents challenges in maintaining a healthy work-life balance. O'Grady has had to navigate the complexities of managing his personal relationships, health, and personal well-being while juggling the demands of his career. Striking this balance requires careful prioritization and self-care, which O'Grady has managed with grace and resilience.

Despite these challenges and setbacks, O'Grady's ability to persevere and overcome adversity has been instrumental in his continued success. His unwavering determination, coupled with his ability to find humor in difficult situations, has allowed him to rise above setbacks and maintain a positive outlook.

It is through these challenges and setbacks that O'Grady's story becomes relatable and inspiring. His ability to navigate through adversity serves as a reminder that setbacks are a natural part of life, and it is how one responds to them that truly matters. O'Grady's resilience and determination are a testament to his character and a source of inspiration for others facing their own challenges.

CHAPTER FOUR

4. The Birth of Lily Savage

The birth of Lily Savage marked a significant turning point in Paul O'Grady's career and introduced a character that would become an iconic figure in the entertainment industry. The creation of Lily Savage stemmed from O'Grady's desire to push boundaries, showcase his comedic talents, and connect with audiences in a unique and memorable way.

The genesis of Lily Savage can be traced back to O'Grady's upbringing in the vibrant city of Liverpool. Influenced by the city's rich cultural scene and colorful characters, O'Grady developed a deep appreciation for comedy and a fascination with drag queens. Inspired by the flamboyant and charismatic drag performers he encountered; O'Grady began experimenting with his own drag persona.

Lily Savage emerged as a larger-than-life character, embodying a brash, quick-witted, and glamorous alter ego. With her sassy personality, extravagant costumes, and razor-sharp tongue, Lily captivated audiences from the moment she took the stage. O'Grady's impeccable comedic timing and ability to seamlessly slip into character brought Lily to life, captivating audiences, and leaving them in stitches.

Lily Savage's popularity soared as she became a regular fixture on the cabaret circuit. Her unique blend of comedy, glamour, and audacity made her a favorite among audiences. Lily's performances were a fusion of sharp wit, hilarious anecdotes, and audience interaction, creating an unforgettable experience for those fortunate enough to witness her act.

As Lily Savage's star continued to rise, O'Grady seized opportunities to bring her to a broader audience. Television appearances showcased Lily's outrageous humor and magnetic stage presence, allowing O'Grady to introduce her to a wider audience. Her appearances on shows such as "The James Whale Radio Show" and "Opportunity Knocks" served as stepping stones, elevating her visibility and paving the way for greater success.

The breakthrough moment for Lily Savage came with her own television show, "The Lily Savage Show," which aired from 1997 to 2000. The show provided a platform for Lily to shine, featuring a mix of comedy sketches, celebrity interviews, and audience interaction. Lily's infectious charm, quick wit, and irreverent humor resonated with viewers, solidifying her status as an iconic comedic character.

The birth of Lily Savage not only propelled O'Grady to new heights of fame but also allowed him to challenge societal norms and push the boundaries of comedy. Lily's unapologetic and audacious persona defied conventional expectations, breaking down barriers and paving the way for a more diverse and inclusive entertainment landscape.

Beyond her comedic prowess, Lily Savage became a cultural icon and a symbol of empowerment. She embodied the spirit of self-expression and showed that authenticity and individuality are to be celebrated. Lily's impact extended beyond the stage, inspiring countless individuals to embrace their true selves and find the courage to express their uniqueness.

The birth of Lily Savage represented a transformative moment in Paul O'Grady's career. Through her creation, O'Grady unleashed a force of comedy and charisma that captivated audiences and left an indelible mark on the entertainment industry. Lily's enduring legacy serves as a testament to O'Grady's talent, creativity, and ability to connect with audiences in a way that transcends boundaries and resonates with the human spirit.

4.1 The creation and development of the iconic drag queen persona

The creation and development of Paul O'Grady's iconic drag queen persona, Lily Savage, is a fascinating journey that showcases O'Grady's creativity, wit, and ability to bring a larger-than-life character to life. The birth and evolution of Lily Savage involved a combination of personal experiences, artistic vision, and a deep understanding of the power of comedy.

The early seeds of Lily Savage were sown during O'Grady's upbringing in Liverpool, where he was exposed to the city's vibrant culture and diverse characters. Inspired by the flamboyant drag queens he encountered in the local scene, O'Grady began experimenting with his own drag persona as a way to express his comedic talents and push the boundaries of traditional comedy.

Drawing inspiration from the strong women in his life and the larger-than-life personalities of Liverpool's working-class communities, O'Grady developed Lily Savage as a character that embodied audacity, wit, and glamour. Lily became an amalgamation of O'Grady's observations, imagination, and desire to create a persona that could captivate and entertain audiences like no other.

The development of Lily Savage involved meticulous attention to detail, from her distinctive makeup and glamorous outfits to her quick-witted banter and cutting humor. O'Grady honed Lily's comedic timing, studied the nuances of drag performance, and drew on his own experiences to shape her into a character that felt authentic and relatable.

As O'Grady delved deeper into Lily Savage's development, he found that she had an incredible ability to connect with audiences. Lily's sharp tongue, irreverent humor, and fearless personality resonated with people from all walks of life. She became a voice for the marginalized and a symbol of empowerment, challenging societal norms and giving a platform to a drag queen character like no other.

The evolution of Lily Savage was not without its challenges. O'Grady faced skepticism and resistance from some quarters, as Lily's audacious and provocative nature pushed the boundaries of traditional comedy. However, O'Grady remained steadfast in his vision, believing in the power of Lily's character to challenge perceptions and bring joy to audiences.

Through stage performances, television appearances, and her own show, Lily Savage became a beloved figure in the entertainment industry. O'Grady's talent for seamlessly embodying Lily's persona, coupled with her sharp wit and larger-than-life presence, propelled her to become an icon of British comedy.

Beyond her entertainment value, Lily Savage's impact went beyond the stage. She helped to break down stereotypes and foster greater acceptance of the LGBTQ+ community. Lily's unapologetic and fearless approach to self-expression inspired countless individuals to embrace their true selves and challenged societal norms regarding gender and identity.

The creation and development of the iconic drag queen persona of Lily Savage represent a defining chapter in Paul O'Grady's career. Through her, O'Grady unleashed a force of comedy, wit, and empowerment that continues to captivate audiences to this day. Lily Savage's legacy as a trailblazing and empowering figure in the entertainment industry is a testament to O'Grady's creative vision, dedication, and ability to create a character that transcends time and leaves an indelible mark on popular culture.

4.2 Lily Savage's Rise to Fame and Popularity

Lily Savage's rise to fame and popularity was a remarkable journey that propelled her from local cabaret circuits to becoming a national phenomenon. With her unique blend of humor, glamour, and audacity, Lily captivated audiences and carved out a special place in the hearts of people across the United Kingdom.

Lily Savage's ascent to stardom began with her captivating stage performances in the vibrant cabaret scene. Her larger-than-life personality, quick wit, and dazzling costumes captured the attention of audiences and earned her a devoted following. Lily's performances were a perfect balance of comedy, storytelling, and audience interaction, creating an unforgettable experience for those fortunate enough to witness her act.

As Lily's popularity grew, she caught the attention of television producers, who recognized her unique talent and potential to entertain a wider audience. Lily Savage made her television debut on "The James Whale Radio Show," where her outrageous humor and magnetic stage presence captivated viewers. This initial exposure paved the way for more significant television appearances, showcasing Lily's comedic prowess to a broader audience.

One of the pivotal moments in Lily Savage's rise to fame was her appearance on the talent show "Opportunity Knocks." Lily's sharp wit, irreverent humor, and ability to engage with the audience propelled her to win the show's viewers' vote, solidifying her status as a rising star. This victory catapulted Lily into the national spotlight, introducing her to a wide range of viewers who were instantly captivated by her larger-than-life persona.

With her newfound fame, Lily Savage's career reached new heights. She became a regular fixture on television shows, appearing in popular programs such as "Blankety Blank" and "Celebrity Squares." Lily's ability to effortlessly connect with both celebrity guests and the audience endeared her to viewers and further boosted her popularity.

The breakthrough moment for Lily Savage came with the launch of her own television show, "The Lily Savage Show," which aired from 1997 to 2000. The show showcased Lily's comedic talents, featuring a mix of comedy sketches, celebrity interviews, and musical performances. Lily's irreverent humor and quick comebacks made the show a hit, attracting a loyal fan base and earning critical acclaim.

"The Lily Savage Show" brought Lily Savage into millions of living rooms across the country, cementing her status as an iconic figure in British entertainment. Her ability to navigate a variety of comedic scenarios and her natural charisma made her a beloved household name. Lily became a symbol of empowerment, unapologetically challenging societal norms and inspiring audiences to embrace their uniqueness.

Beyond television, Lily Savage's popularity extended to other media platforms. She published a successful autobiography titled "Lily Savage: The Autobiography," which further endeared her to fans. Lily also embarked on successful stage shows and live tours, captivating audiences with her electrifying performances and trademark humor.

Lily Savage's rise to fame and popularity was a testament to her exceptional comedic talents, captivating stage presence, and the unique connection she forged with audiences. Her audacious personality, quick wit, and empowering message resonated with people from all walks of life, establishing Lily as a beloved and enduring icon in the entertainment industry.

4.3 Behind-the-scenes Stories and Anecdotes

Behind the glamorous persona of Lily Savage, there are numerous intriguing behind-the-scenes stories and anecdotes that shed light on the person behind the character, Paul O'Grady. These stories reveal the wit, resilience, and charm that have contributed to Lily Savage's enduring appeal.

1. The Creation of Lily's Outrageous Outfits: One fascinating aspect of Lily Savage's character was her extravagant costumes. Behind the scenes, O'Grady was heavily involved in designing and creating these elaborate outfits. He often sourced materials collaborated with costume designers, and even constructed some of the garments himself. These behind-the-scenes efforts ensured that Lily's appearance was always striking and perfectly complemented her larger-than-life personality.

2. Improvisation and Quick Thinking: Lily Savage's quick wit and ability to engage with the audience were legendary. Many of the humorous moments and one-liners were a result of O'Grady's improvisation skills. He had an innate ability to react at the moment, adapt to unexpected situations, and deliver hilarious responses on the fly. This talent for improvisation added an element of unpredictability to Lily's performances, keeping both the audience and fellow performers on their toes.

3. The Art of Banter: Lily Savage's interactions with the audience were a hallmark of her shows. She had a knack for playful banter, often teasing audience members in good humor. These interactions created an electric atmosphere and allowed Lily to showcase her razor-sharp wit. Behind the scenes, O'Grady honed this skill through years of experience and developed an intuitive sense of how to engage with the crowd and keep them entertained.

4. Maintaining Composure during Mishaps: Like any live performance, Lily Savage's shows were not immune to the occasional mishap. From wardrobe malfunctions to technical glitches, unforeseen challenges

would sometimes arise. However, O'Grady's professionalism and composure in such situations were remarkable. He would effortlessly incorporate these mishaps into the act, turning them into comedic moments that left audiences in stitches. O'Grady's ability to remain poised and turn potential disasters into memorable comedic moments was a testament to his talent and adaptability.

5. Backstage Camaraderie: Behind the scenes, Lily Savage was known for fostering a warm and inclusive environment. O'Grady, along with the crew and fellow performers, created a close-knit community. Stories of backstage camaraderie, laughter-filled dressing rooms, and shared experiences highlight the supportive and collaborative atmosphere that contributed to the success of Lily's shows. O'Grady's infectious energy and genuine appreciation for the people he worked with helped cultivate a positive and uplifting environment.

6. Making a Difference: Beyond the glamour and laughter, Lily Savage's impact extended beyond the stage. O'Grady used his platform to raise awareness and support charitable causes, particularly those related to LGBTQ+ rights and HIV/AIDS. His tireless advocacy work, both in and out of drag, demonstrated his compassion and commitment to making a difference in the lives of others.

These behind-the-scenes stories and anecdotes provide a glimpse into the world of Lily Savage and the remarkable individual behind the character, Paul O'Grady. They reveal the dedication, talent, and genuine passion that have made Lily Savage an enduring icon of comedy and empowerment.

CHAPTER FIVE

5. TV Shows and Beyond

Throughout Paul O'Grady's career, both as himself and as Lily Savage, he has ventured into various television shows and other endeavors, showcasing his versatility and ability to connect with audiences across different formats. Here are some notable TV shows and ventures that have played a significant role in O'Grady's journey:

1. "The Paul O'Grady Show": After the success of Lily Savage, O'Grady transitioned to hosting his own talk show, "The Paul O'Grady Show." Running from 2004 to 2009, and later returning in 2013, the show featured a mix of celebrity interviews, musical performances, and comedic sketches. O'Grady's charm, wit, and genuine rapport with guests endeared him to viewers and made the show a hit.

2. "For the Love of Dogs": O'Grady's love for animals led to his involvement in the heartwarming reality TV series "For the Love of Dogs." The show, which began in 2012, follows O'Grady as he visits and interacts with dogs in animal rescue centers. His compassion and genuine connection with the animals resonated with audiences, making the show immensely popular.

3. "Blankety Blank": O'Grady stepped into the shoes of the legendary game show host Terry Wogan when he hosted the revived version of "Blankety Blank" in 1997. The show, known for its humorous fill-in-the-blank questions, allowed O'Grady to showcase his comedic timing and engage with celebrity contestants and the audience.

4. "An Audience with Paul O'Grady": In 2006, O'Grady had the opportunity to headline his own special comedy show, "An Audience with Paul O'Grady." The show featured a mix of stand-up comedy, celebrity interviews, and musical performances, giving O'Grady a platform to showcase his comedic talents and connect with his audience in a more intimate setting.

5. Theater and Stage Performances: O'Grady's talents have extended beyond television. He has appeared in numerous theater productions, including playing the role of the Child Catcher in the West End production of "Chitty Chitty Bang Bang" and the role of Captain Hook in "Peter Pan." His stage performances allowed him to showcase his versatility as a performer and entertain audiences in a different setting.

6. Writing and Autobiography: O'Grady's talent for storytelling is not limited to his performances on stage and screen. He has also ventured into writing, with his autobiography "At My Mother's Knee...and Other Low Joints" becoming a bestseller. In the book, O'Grady shares intimate details of his life, including his childhood, career, and personal experiences, providing readers with a deeper understanding of the man behind the iconic characters.

Beyond television, O'Grady has used his platform to support various charitable causes. He has been an advocate for LGBTQ+ rights and has worked closely with organizations focused on HIV/AIDS awareness and support. O'Grady's dedication to making a positive impact and his commitment to using his influence for the greater good has further endeared him to audiences and solidified his legacy as a beloved entertainer.

These TV shows and ventures reflect Paul O'Grady's diverse range of talents, his ability to entertain across different mediums, and his enduring connection with audiences. Whether as himself or through the iconic character of Lily Savage, O'Grady has left an indelible mark on the world of entertainment, captivating viewers with his wit, charm, and genuine passion for his craft.

5.1 Hosting Roles and television appearances

Paul O'Grady has taken on various hosting roles and made numerous television appearances throughout his career, showcasing his versatility and endearing personality. Here are some notable hosting roles and television appearances that have contributed to O'Grady's success:

1. "The Paul O'Grady Show" (2004-2009, 2013): As the host of his own talk show, O'Grady charmed audiences with his engaging interviews, entertaining banter, and humorous sketches. The show featured celebrity guests, live music performances, and comedy segments, allowing O'Grady to showcase his wit and ability to connect with guests and viewers.

2. "Paul O'Grady's Animal Orphans" (2014-2015): This heartwarming documentary series followed O'Grady as he visited animal rescue centers and encountered orphaned animals in need of care and rehabilitation. O'Grady's compassion and genuine love for animals shone through in his hosting, making the show a hit with animal lovers.

3. "Paul O'Grady: For the Love of Dogs" (2012-present): This immensely popular series followed O'Grady as he visited Battersea Dogs & Cats Home, interacting with and caring for the dogs in need of forever homes. O'Grady's genuine connection with the animals and his infectious enthusiasm resonated with viewers, making the show a beloved fixture of British television.

4. "The British Soap Awards": O'Grady has hosted "The British Soap Awards" multiple times, bringing his unique sense of humor and charm to the annual event honoring the best of British soap operas. His hosting style and comedic timing added an extra layer of entertainment to the star-studded ceremony.

5. Guest Appearances: O'Grady has made numerous guest appearances on various television shows, including comedy panel shows like "Would I Lie to You?" and "8 Out of 10 Cats." His quick wit and

engaging personality have made him a sought-after guest, bringing laughter and lively conversation to the shows he appears on.

6. Awards Show Hosting: O'Grady has hosted several awards shows throughout his career, including the National Television Awards and the British Comedy Awards. His ability to entertain large audiences and keep the energy high has made him a natural choice for hosting such prestigious events.

These hosting roles and television appearances highlight O'Grady's ability to connect with audiences, whether through interviews, comedy sketches, or his genuine love for animals. His warmth, wit, and down-to-earth persona have made him a beloved figure in British television, and his hosting abilities have solidified his status as an exceptional entertainer.

5.2 Notable Collaborations and Projects

Paul O'Grady has had the opportunity to collaborate with various notable individuals and engage in exciting projects throughout his career. Here are some of his notable collaborations and projects:

1. Collaboration with Cilla Black: O'Grady and the late Cilla Black, a beloved British entertainer, had a close friendship and frequently worked together. They collaborated on various television shows, including "Surprise, Surprise," where O'Grady stepped in as a guest presenter on several occasions. Their on-screen chemistry and shared sense of humor made for memorable moments and endeared them to audiences.

2. Collaboration with Amanda Holden: O'Grady and Amanda Holden, an actress and television personality, have enjoyed a successful collaboration. They co-hosted the ITV show "Paul O'Grady's Saturday Night" in 2008, showcasing their chemistry and comedic timing. Their

partnership brought laughter and entertainment to viewers, establishing a dynamic duo on screen.

3. Collaboration with Richard Ayoade: O'Grady collaborated with the talented comedian and presenter Richard Ayoade on the comedy panel show "Travel Man: 48 Hours In..." In the episode featuring Istanbul, O'Grady joined Ayoade as they embarked on an adventure exploring the city. Their contrasting personalities and humorous interactions made for an entertaining and enjoyable episode.

4. Collaboration with BBC Radio 2: O'Grady has been a guest presenter on BBC Radio 2, hosting his own show and sharing his eclectic taste in music. His warm and engaging style translated well to radio, allowing him to connect with listeners and share stories, anecdotes, and his love for music.

5. The Lily Savage Books: O'Grady collaborated with renowned writer and journalist Christopher Biggins on the Lily Savage book series. Together, they brought Lily's iconic personality and humor to the written page, delighting fans with hilarious anecdotes, outrageous stories, and insights into Lily's world.

6. Philanthropic Work: O'Grady has also collaborated with various charitable organizations and initiatives. He has been involved in fundraising efforts for causes such as HIV/AIDS research and support, children's charities, and animal welfare. O'Grady's commitment to making a positive impact and using his influence for good has led to meaningful collaborations that have made a difference in people's lives.

These notable collaborations and projects demonstrate O'Grady's ability to work alongside talented individuals, creating entertaining and impactful content. From on-screen partnerships to charitable endeavors, O'Grady's collaborations have enriched his career and contributed to his enduring popularity as an entertainer.

5.3 Exploring other creative avenues

In addition to his successful career in television and hosting, Paul O'Grady has explored various other creative avenues, showcasing his versatility and passion for the arts. Here are some examples of his ventures into different creative realms:

1. Writing: O'Grady has demonstrated his talent as a writer through his autobiographical works. His memoirs, such as "At My Mother's Knee...and Other Low Joints," provide readers with a candid and heartfelt account of his life, including personal anecdotes, reflections, and humorous stories. O'Grady's writing style captures his unique voice and allows readers to delve deeper into his experiences and perspectives.

2. Acting: O'Grady has ventured into the world of acting, showcasing his versatility on stage and screen. He has taken on roles in theater productions, including performances in plays such as "Prick Up Your Ears" and "Cabaret." O'Grady's acting talents have allowed him to explore different characters and bring his comedic timing and dramatic flair to new artistic realms.

3. Stand-Up Comedy: Before his television career took off, O'Grady honed his comedic skills on the stand-up comedy circuit. He performed in comedy clubs, festivals, and theaters, delivering his unique brand of humor to audiences. O'Grady's ability to captivate and entertain audiences with his witty observations and engaging storytelling has been a constant throughout his career.

4. Voice Acting: O'Grady has lent his distinctive voice to various animated projects. His voice-acting credits include characters in animated films and TV shows, bringing his charm and charisma to the world of animation. His vocal talent adds a new dimension to his creative repertoire and showcases his ability to bring characters to life through his voice alone.

5. Artistic Endeavors: O'Grady has also expressed his creativity through artistic endeavors, including painting. He has shared his artwork with the public, allowing audiences to appreciate his talent and artistic expression beyond his work in entertainment. O'Grady's artistic pursuits highlight his multidimensional nature and his desire to explore different forms of self-expression.

6. Music: O'Grady has occasionally showcased his musical talents, particularly through his love for singing. Whether performing a musical number on his talk show or participating in charity events, he has delighted audiences with his vocal abilities. His passion for music adds yet another layer to his creative repertoire.

These ventures into writing, acting, stand-up comedy, voice acting, art, and music demonstrate Paul O'Grady's willingness to explore different creative avenues and push the boundaries of his artistic pursuits. His versatility and passion for the arts have allowed him to connect with audiences on various levels, showcasing his immense talent and bringing joy to fans across different mediums.

CHAPTER SIX

6. Philanthropy and Activism

Paul O'Grady has been actively involved in philanthropy and activism throughout his career, using his platform and influence to support various charitable causes and advocate for social change. Here are some examples of his philanthropic efforts and activism:

1. LGBTQ+ Advocacy: O'Grady has been an outspoken advocate for LGBTQ+ rights and visibility. As an openly gay public figure, he has used his platform to raise awareness about LGBTQ+ issues and promote acceptance and equality. O'Grady has lent his support to organizations such as Stonewall, a leading LGBTQ+ rights charity in the UK, and has spoken publicly about the importance of LGBTQ+ representation in the media and society.

2. HIV/AIDS Awareness: O'Grady has been actively involved in raising awareness and supporting organizations focused on HIV/AIDS research, prevention, and support. He has participated in fundraising events, including hosting the Stonewall Equality Show in support of the Elton John AIDS Foundation. O'Grady's efforts have helped shed light on the ongoing challenges faced by those affected by HIV/AIDS and the importance of continued support and research.

3. Animal Welfare: O'Grady's love for animals is well-known, and he has been involved in various initiatives to promote animal welfare and advocate for the rights and well-being of animals. His work with Battersea Dogs & Cats Home, as showcased in the TV series "Paul O'Grady: For the Love of Dogs," has helped raise awareness about the importance of animal adoption and responsible pet ownership. O'Grady has also supported other animal charities, including the RSPCA and the Dogs Trust.

4. Children's Charities: O'Grady has actively supported children's charities and initiatives, recognizing the importance of providing

support and opportunities for disadvantaged children. He has been involved in fundraising events for organizations such as Children in Need, which aims to improve the lives of children in the UK facing challenges such as poverty, illness, and disability. O'Grady's involvement has helped raise vital funds for programs and services benefiting children in need.

5. Fundraising Events and Telethons: O'Grady has lent his time and talent to various fundraising events and telethons, using his comedic abilities and genuine charm to encourage donations and support important causes. He has hosted segments of telethons such as Red Nose Day, which raises funds for Comic Relief's charitable projects tackling poverty and social injustice. O'Grady's involvement has helped generate significant contributions and make a positive impact on numerous charitable initiatives.

Through his philanthropic efforts and activism, Paul O'Grady has demonstrated a genuine commitment to making a difference in the lives of others. His advocacy for LGBTQ+ rights, support for HIV/AIDS research and awareness, dedication to animal welfare, and involvement in children's charities have highlighted his compassion, empathy, and desire to create positive change. O'Grady's contributions to philanthropy and activism have made a significant impact, inspiring others to get involved and contribute to causes they care about.

6.1 Paul O'Grady's Involvement in charitable causes

Paul O'Grady has been actively involved in supporting charitable causes throughout his career, demonstrating his dedication to making a positive impact in the lives of others. Here are some examples of his involvement in charitable endeavors:

1. Battersea Dogs & Cats Home: O'Grady's passion for animals led him to become closely associated with Battersea Dogs & Cats Home, a renowned animal rescue organization in the UK. He has been a patron

of the charity for many years and has actively supported their work in finding loving homes for abandoned and mistreated animals. O'Grady's involvement includes hosting the popular TV series "Paul O'Grady: For the Love of Dogs," which showcases the heartwarming stories of the animals at Battersea and raises awareness about responsible pet ownership.

2. HIV/AIDS Charities: O'Grady has been an advocate for HIV/AIDS charities and has actively participated in fundraising events to support organizations working in this field. He has used his platform to raise awareness about the ongoing challenges faced by individuals living with HIV/AIDS and the importance of prevention, research, and support. O'Grady's involvement has helped generate funds for initiatives focused on education, treatment, and care for those affected by the disease.

3. Children's Charities: O'Grady has been committed to improving the lives of children facing adversity. He has supported various children's charities, including Children in Need, which provides funding to projects that address the needs of disadvantaged children across the UK. O'Grady's involvement in fundraising events and his support for initiatives aimed at improving the well-being and opportunities for children have made a significant impact on the lives of those in need.

4. LGBTQ+ Rights and Advocacy: As an openly gay public figure, O'Grady has been a strong advocate for LGBTQ+ rights and visibility. He has used his platform to speak out against discrimination, promote acceptance, and raise awareness about the challenges faced by the LGBTQ+ community. O'Grady has supported organizations such as Stonewall, which works toward achieving equality for LGBTQ+ individuals and has actively participated in events aimed at promoting LGBTQ+ rights and awareness.

5. Fundraising Events and Telethons: O'Grady has lent his time and talent to various fundraising events and telethons, using his humor and charisma to encourage donations and support for charitable causes. He has hosted segments of telethons like Red Nose Day and has been

involved in initiatives to raise funds for projects tackling poverty, illness, and social injustice. O'Grady's participation in these events has helped generate substantial contributions for charitable organizations and initiatives.

Through his involvement in charitable causes, Paul O'Grady has demonstrated a genuine commitment to making a positive difference. His support for animal welfare, HIV/AIDS research, children's charities, LGBTQ+ rights, and various fundraising initiatives have had a significant impact on the lives of individuals and communities in need. O'Grady's philanthropic endeavors have not only raised awareness and funds but also inspired others to get involved and support causes close to their hearts.

6.2 Advocacy Work and Contributions to Society

Paul O'Grady has made significant contributions to society through his advocacy work and efforts to promote positive change. Here are some examples of his advocacy work and contributions:

1. LGBTQ+ Advocacy: As an openly gay public figure, O'Grady has been a strong advocate for LGBTQ+ rights and visibility. He has used his platform to raise awareness about LGBTQ+ issues, challenge stereotypes, and promote acceptance. O'Grady's visibility and candid discussions about his own experiences have helped foster understanding and support for the LGBTQ+ community.

2. Mental Health Awareness: O'Grady has been vocal about his own struggles with mental health, particularly with depression. By openly discussing his experiences, he has helped reduce the stigma surrounding mental health issues and encouraged others to seek help and support. O'Grady's honesty and vulnerability have provided comfort and inspiration to those facing similar challenges.

3. Community Support: O'Grady has actively supported local communities and grassroots initiatives. He has championed the importance of community spirit and has been involved in projects that promote unity, solidarity, and positive change at the local level. O'Grady's efforts have helped strengthen communities and improve the lives of individuals within them.

4. Elderly Care and Support: O'Grady has been an advocate for improving the care and support provided to elderly individuals. He has highlighted the challenges faced by older people, including isolation and neglect, and has called for increased resources and attention to address these issues. O'Grady's advocacy has helped shed light on the importance of caring for and valuing our older population.

5. Charity Fundraising: O'Grady has actively participated in charity fundraising efforts, using his influence to generate support and donations for various charitable causes. Whether through hosting events, participating in telethons, or engaging in personal fundraising initiatives, he has played a vital role in raising funds for organizations addressing social issues and providing support to vulnerable individuals.

6. Inspiring Others: O'Grady's openness, compassion, and dedication to making a positive impact have inspired countless individuals. Through his advocacy work and personal contributions, he has motivated others to get involved, speak out about important issues, and take action to create positive change in their own communities.

Paul O'Grady's advocacy work and contributions to society have been significant. His efforts to promote LGBTQ+ rights, raise awareness about mental health, support local communities, advocate for the elderly, and actively participate in charity fundraising have made a lasting impact on individuals and communities. O'Grady's dedication to improving lives and inspiring others serves as a powerful example of the positive influence one person can have on society.

6.3 Impact and Recognition for philanthropic efforts

Paul O'Grady's philanthropic efforts have had a significant impact on various causes and have garnered recognition for his dedication to making a difference in the lives of others. Here are some examples of the impact and recognition he has received for his philanthropic work:

1. Increased Awareness and Support: O'Grady's involvement in charitable causes has helped raise awareness about important issues and generated increased support for organizations and initiatives. Through his advocacy, he has brought attention to issues such as animal welfare, HIV/AIDS, LGBTQ+ rights, and children's charities, leading to greater public awareness and support for these causes.

2. Fundraising Success: O'Grady's participation in fundraising events and telethons has contributed to significant fundraising successes. His involvement and endorsement have encouraged others to donate and contribute to charitable initiatives, resulting in substantial funds raised for various organizations and projects. O'Grady's charisma and ability to connect with people have undoubtedly played a role in the success of these fundraising efforts.

3. Impact on Beneficiaries: O'Grady's support for charitable causes has directly impacted the lives of individuals and communities in need. Whether through providing care and shelter for abandoned animals, funding research and support for those affected by HIV/AIDS, or improving the lives of disadvantaged children, his contributions have made a tangible difference in the lives of beneficiaries.

4. Awards and Recognition: O'Grady's philanthropic efforts have been recognized and honored with various awards. His commitment to animal welfare led to him receiving the Special Recognition Award from the Battersea Dogs & Cats Home for his work in raising awareness and supporting the organization. Additionally, O'Grady has been

recognized for his contributions to the LGBTQ+ community, receiving accolades and acknowledgments for his advocacy and support.

5. Inspiration and Influence: O'Grady's philanthropic work has inspired others to get involved and make a positive impact in their own communities. His dedication and passion have motivated individuals to support charitable causes, volunteer their time, and become advocates for important issues. O'Grady's influence extends beyond his own efforts, as he has encouraged a broader movement of compassion and social responsibility.

The impact and recognition Paul O'Grady has received for his philanthropic efforts underscore the significance of his contributions to society. His work has raised awareness, generated support, and directly improved the lives of individuals and communities. Through his dedication to making a positive difference and inspiring others, O'Grady's philanthropy serves as a testament to the power of compassion and generosity in creating meaningful change.

CHAPTER SEVEN

7. Personal Life and Relationships

Paul O'Grady's personal life and relationships have played an important role in shaping his experiences and worldview. While respecting O'Grady's privacy, here is a brief overview of his personal life and relationships:

1. Relationships: O'Grady has had significant relationships throughout his life. He was in a long-term relationship with Brendan Murphy, who sadly passed away in 2005. O'Grady has spoken fondly of their time together and the impact Brendan had on his life. O'Grady has also mentioned his close relationship with his mother and how her influence shaped his values and outlook.

2. Parenting: O'Grady is a father to a daughter, Sharyn, whom he had with his former girlfriend, Diane Jansen. Despite the challenges of being a public figure, O'Grady has been dedicated to his role as a parent and has spoken about the joy and fulfillment he experiences in his relationship with his daughter.

3. Privacy: O'Grady is known for maintaining a relatively private personal life. He has chosen to keep certain aspects of his relationships and personal experiences out of the public eye, valuing his privacy and the privacy of those close to him.

4. Love for Animals: O'Grady's love for animals is well-known and has been an integral part of his personal life. He has shared his home with several beloved pets over the years and has been a passionate advocate for animal welfare.

5. Balancing Personal and Professional Life: O'Grady has faced the challenge of balancing his personal and professional life, navigating the demands of his career while maintaining meaningful relationships and

personal well-being. He has been open about the importance of finding a balance and prioritizing self-care.

It's important to respect O'Grady's privacy when discussing his personal life and relationships. While he has shared some aspects of his personal experiences publicly, it's crucial to recognize that he is entitled to maintain boundaries and keep certain details private.

7.1 Insights into Paul O'Grady's personal relationships

Paul O'Grady has been quite private about his personal relationships, and he prefers to keep the details of his romantic life out of the public eye. While he has spoken openly about his long-term relationship with Brendan Murphy, who sadly passed away in 2005, and has expressed deep affection and gratitude for their time together, O'Grady has not extensively discussed subsequent romantic relationships.

O'Grady has also mentioned his close relationship with his daughter, Sharyn, whom he had with his former girlfriend, Diane Jansen. He has spoken about the joy and fulfillment he experiences as a father and the importance of their bond. However, he typically keeps his daughter's life away from the spotlight to respect her privacy.

Throughout his career, O'Grady has emphasized the significance of his family, particularly his mother, who has had a profound influence on his life. He has spoken fondly of their relationship and the values instilled in him by his mother.

It's important to respect O'Grady's choice to maintain privacy regarding his personal relationships. As a public figure, he has the right to keep certain aspects of his personal life separate from his public persona. By respecting his boundaries, we allow him the freedom to share what he feels comfortable with while preserving his privacy and that of his loved ones.

7.2 Key Milestones and significant events

Paul O'Grady's life has been marked by various key milestones and significant events that have shaped his personal and professional journey. Here are some notable milestones and events in his life:

1. Birth and Early Years: Paul O'Grady was born on June 14, 1955, in Birkenhead, England. His upbringing in a working-class family laid the foundation for his down-to-earth demeanor and sense of humor.

2. Early Career in Entertainment: O'Grady began his career in entertainment in the 1970s, initially performing as a drag queen in various clubs. These early experiences helped shape his unique persona and comedic style.

3. The Birth of Lily Savage: One of the defining moments in O'Grady's career was the creation of his iconic drag queen alter ego, Lily Savage. Lily Savage became a beloved character known for her sharp wit, outrageous fashion, and quick comebacks.

4. Stand-Up Comedy Success: O'Grady gained recognition as a stand-up comedian in the 1980s and '90s, earning a reputation for his hilarious performances and ability to connect with audiences.

5. Television Breakthrough: O'Grady's television career took off with the success of "The Paul O'Grady Show" in the early 2000s. The talk show, which featured celebrity interviews, comedy sketches, and music performances, became a hit and earned him widespread popularity.

6. Animal Welfare Advocacy: O'Grady's passion for animals led him to become closely associated with Battersea Dogs & Cats Home. His involvement with the organization, including hosting the TV series

"Paul O'Grady: For the Love of Dogs," highlighted his commitment to animal welfare and raised awareness about the importance of responsible pet ownership.

7. Literary Success: O'Grady has authored several books, including autobiographical works such as "At My Mother's Knee... and Other Low Joints" and "The Devil Rides Out," which have been well-received by readers and further showcased his storytelling abilities.

8. Philanthropic Contributions: O'Grady's dedication to philanthropy and advocacy work has been a consistent theme throughout his life. His involvement with charitable causes, including HIV/AIDS charities, children's charities, and LGBTQ+ rights organizations, has made a significant impact and earned him recognition for his contributions.

9. Television Hosting and Guest Appearances: O'Grady has hosted various television programs, including game shows, award ceremonies, and documentaries. He has also made guest appearances on numerous TV shows, further solidifying his presence in the entertainment industry.

10. Awards and Honors: O'Grady's talent and contributions have been acknowledged with numerous awards and honors throughout his career. These include multiple National Television Awards, British Comedy Awards, and recognition for his charity work.

These key milestones and significant events represent the diverse and impactful journey of Paul O'Grady's life and career. Each experience has contributed to his growth as an entertainer, philanthropist, and advocate for causes close to his heart.

7.3 Balancing Fame and personal life

Balancing fame and personal life can be a challenge for individuals in the public eye, including Paul O'Grady. While O'Grady has been open about certain aspects of his personal life, he has also made a conscious effort to maintain boundaries and protect his privacy. Here are some insights into how he has navigated the balance between fame and personal life:

1. Setting Boundaries: O'Grady understands the importance of setting boundaries between his public persona and personal life. He has chosen to keep certain aspects of his relationships and personal experiences private, allowing him to maintain a sense of normalcy and protect the privacy of his loved ones.

2. Prioritizing Personal Time: Despite his busy schedule and public commitments, O'Grady recognizes the significance of personal time and ensuring a healthy work-life balance. He has expressed the importance of taking breaks, spending time with family and friends, and engaging in activities outside of the spotlight.

3. Keeping Relationships Private: O'Grady has generally kept his romantic relationships away from the public eye. By maintaining privacy in this area, he has been able to foster meaningful connections without the added pressures and scrutiny that come with being a public figure.

4. Valuing Authenticity: O'Grady has always prioritized authenticity in his career and personal life. By staying true to himself and his values, he has been able to navigate fame without compromising his sense of self.

5. Seeking Support: Like anyone in the public eye, O'Grady understands the importance of having a support system. He has surrounded himself with trusted friends, family, and colleagues who provide him with the support and guidance needed to navigate the challenges of fame.

6. Establishing Offline Moments: O'Grady has emphasized the importance of having offline moments, away from the constant presence of technology and social media. Disconnecting from the virtual world allows him to focus on personal connections and recharge away from the demands of fame.

7. Protecting Loved Ones: O'Grady has taken measures to shield his loved ones from unwanted attention and scrutiny. By keeping their lives private, he ensures their well-being and minimizes the intrusion of fame into their personal lives.

Balancing fame and personal life is an ongoing process, and each individual navigates it in their own way. For Paul O'Grady, maintaining boundaries, prioritizing personal time, valuing authenticity, seeking support, and protecting loved ones have been key strategies in striking a balance between his public and private spheres. By finding a harmonious equilibrium, O'Grady has been able to preserve his personal life while enjoying a successful career in the public eye.

CHAPTER EIGHT

8. Challenges and Triumphs

Paul O'Grady's life and career have been marked by both challenges and triumphs. Here are some notable challenges he has faced and triumphs he has achieved:

Challenges:

1. Personal Loss: One of the significant challenges in O'Grady's life was the loss of his longtime partner, Brendan Murphy, in 2005. The loss deeply affected O'Grady, and he has spoken about the grief and difficulties he experienced during that time.

2. Health Struggles: O'Grady has faced health challenges throughout his life. He has battled heart problems and has undergone heart surgery. These health issues have required him to take breaks from his work and focus on his well-being.

3. Balancing Fame and Privacy: Being a public figure comes with its own set of challenges, including constant scrutiny and invasion of privacy. O'Grady has had to navigate the balancing act of maintaining his privacy while still engaging with his audience and fulfilling professional commitments.

4. Media Criticism: Like many celebrities, O'Grady has faced criticism from the media at various points in his career. The tabloid culture and intense public scrutiny can be challenging to deal with, requiring resilience and strength to overcome.

Triumphs:

1. Successful Entertainment Career: O'Grady's entertainment career has been a triumph in itself. From his early days as a drag queen to becoming

a renowned television personality, comedian, and writer, he has achieved significant success in the entertainment industry.

2. Creation of Iconic Characters: O'Grady's creation of the iconic drag queen character, Lily Savage, brought him widespread recognition and acclaim. Lily Savage became a beloved figure in British entertainment and contributed to O'Grady's rise to fame.

3. Television Success: O'Grady's television shows, such as "The Paul O'Grady Show" and "Paul O'Grady: For the Love of Dogs," have been highly successful and have garnered a loyal fan base. His ability to connect with audiences and deliver entertaining content has been a triumph in his career.

4. Philanthropic Contributions: O'Grady's philanthropic work and advocacy for various causes, including animal welfare and LGBTQ+ rights, have made a significant impact and brought about positive change. His dedication to giving back and making a difference in the lives of others is a triumph in itself.

5. Recognition and Awards: O'Grady has received numerous accolades and awards for his contributions to the entertainment industry and philanthropy. These recognitions highlight the impact he has had and the respect he has garnered throughout his career.

Despite the challenges he has faced, Paul O'Grady's triumphs and successes speak to his resilience, talent, and determination. His ability to overcome obstacles and achieve greatness in his career and philanthropic endeavors is a testament to his character and passion for making a positive impact.

8.1 Overcoming Personal and professional challenges

Paul O'Grady has demonstrated resilience and determination in overcoming personal and professional challenges throughout his life. Here are some examples of how he has faced and conquered these challenges:

1. Grief and Loss: The loss of his partner, Brendan Murphy, was a devastating personal challenge for O'Grady. However, he has shown strength in navigating through his grief, finding ways to honor Murphy's memory, and continuing to move forward in his life and career.

2. Health Struggles: O'Grady's health issues, particularly his heart problems, have presented significant challenges. However, he has taken proactive steps to prioritize his health, undergo necessary medical treatments, and make lifestyle changes to ensure his well-being. By managing his health and seeking appropriate medical care, he has been able to continue pursuing his passions.

3. Balancing Fame and Privacy: Being a public figure comes with its share of challenges in maintaining personal privacy. O'Grady has faced this challenge head-on by setting boundaries, guarding his personal life, and selectively sharing aspects of his experiences. He has found a way to strike a balance that allows him to thrive professionally while preserving his personal life away from the public eye.

4. Media Scrutiny and Criticism: O'Grady has experienced media scrutiny and criticism at various points in his career. However, he has remained resilient and focused on his work, not letting negative comments deter him from pursuing his creative endeavors. He has chosen to rise above the negativity and focus on the positive impact he can make through his talents and philanthropy.

5. Work-Life Balance: Juggling a demanding career with personal commitments can be a challenge for anyone, especially someone in the entertainment industry. O'Grady has navigated this challenge by

recognizing the importance of personal time, setting boundaries, and finding moments of rest and rejuvenation. By prioritizing self-care and maintaining a healthy work-life balance, he has been able to sustain his success and well-being.

6. Turning Setbacks into Opportunities: O'Grady has shown resilience by viewing setbacks as opportunities for growth and learning. When faced with challenges, he has used them as motivation to adapt, evolve, and explore new avenues. This adaptability has allowed him to expand his creative horizons and achieve success in different facets of his career.

Throughout his life, Paul O'Grady has exemplified resilience, determination, and the ability to overcome personal and professional challenges. By facing adversity head-on, he has emerged stronger, wiser, and more committed to his craft and the causes he holds dear. His ability to persevere and find strength in difficult times is a testament to his character and serves as an inspiration to others facing their own challenges.

8.2 Achievements and milestones throughout the years

Paul O'Grady has achieved numerous milestones and notable accomplishments throughout his career. Here are some of his significant achievements over the years:

1. Comedy and Entertainment:
   - Established himself as a successful stand-up comedian in the 1980s and '90s, captivating audiences with his wit and humor.
   - Created the iconic drag queen character, Lily Savage, who became a beloved figure in the entertainment industry and brought O'Grady widespread recognition.

2. Television Success:

- Hosted his own talk show, "The Paul O'Grady Show," from 2004 to 2009, which garnered high ratings and made him a household name in the UK.
- Hosted and appeared in numerous television programs, including game shows, documentaries, and travel shows, showcasing his versatility as a television personality.
- Hosted the critically acclaimed series "Paul O'Grady: For the Love of Dogs," where he showcased his love for animals and raised awareness about animal welfare issues.

3. Writing and Literary Success:

- Authored several successful books, including autobiographical works and children's books, which have resonated with readers and showcased his storytelling abilities.
- Received praise for his writing style and the ability to engage readers with his candid and humorous anecdotes.

4. Philanthropy and Advocacy:

- Demonstrated a strong commitment to philanthropy, particularly in the areas of animal welfare, HIV/AIDS charities, children's charities, and LGBTQ+ rights.
- Supported and raised funds for various charitable organizations, including Battersea Dogs & Cats Home, where he actively participated in promoting responsible pet ownership and finding loving homes for animals in need.

5. Awards and Recognition:

- Received numerous awards and accolades throughout his career, including several National Television Awards, British Comedy Awards, and awards for his philanthropic contributions.
- Honored for his significant contributions to the entertainment industry and charitable endeavors, reflecting the impact he has made in his field.

6. Cultural Influence:

- O'Grady's unique personality and comedic talent have left a lasting impact on British popular culture.
- His drag queen persona, Lily Savage, has become an iconic character and a symbol of British comedy.
- Known for his sharp wit, relatable charm, and ability to connect with audiences, O'Grady has gained a loyal fan base and inspired many aspiring entertainers.

These achievements and milestones highlight the breadth of Paul O'Grady's career and the positive impact he has made as a comedian, television host, writer, philanthropist, and advocate. His contributions to the entertainment industry and his dedication to charitable causes have solidified his status as a respected figure in the UK and beyond.

8.3 Lessons Learned and Growth as an Individual

Throughout his life and career, Paul O'Grady has undoubtedly experienced personal growth and learned valuable lessons. Here are some of the key lessons he may have learned and the growth he has undergone as an individual:

1. Authenticity and Self-Acceptance: O'Grady's journey as a drag queen and his creation of the character Lily Savage have taught him the importance of embracing his true self and celebrating his uniqueness. Through this experience, he has likely learned the value of authenticity and self-acceptance, encouraging others to do the same.

2. Resilience and Perseverance: O'Grady has faced personal and professional challenges throughout his life, including the loss of his partner and health issues. These experiences have likely taught him the importance of resilience and perseverance, enabling him to overcome obstacles and continue pursuing his passions.

3. Compassion and Empathy: O'Grady's involvement in philanthropy, particularly in supporting animal welfare and LGBTQ+ rights, has

likely deepened his sense of compassion and empathy. Through his work and interactions with various communities, he has likely learned the importance of understanding and empathizing with the struggles of others.

4. Balancing Fame and Privacy: Being in the public eye requires navigating the delicate balance between fame and privacy. O'Grady's experiences have likely taught him the significance of setting boundaries, protecting his personal life, and finding ways to maintain a sense of normalcy amidst the demands of his career.

5. Importance of Humor and Laughter: O'Grady's comedic talent and ability to make people laugh have likely taught him the transformative power of humor. He has likely recognized the importance of bringing joy to others and using laughter as a means of connecting with people.

6. Growth Through Personal Loss: The loss of his partner, Brendan Murphy, has likely been a profound catalyst for personal growth. This experience may have taught O'Grady the fragility of life, the value of cherishing relationships, and the resilience required to heal and move forward.

7. Appreciation for Support Systems: O'Grady has likely learned the importance of surrounding himself with a strong support system, including friends, family, and colleagues. He has likely recognized the impact of having people who believe in him and provide support during challenging times.

8. Evolution and Adaptability: Throughout his career, O'Grady has shown a willingness to evolve and adapt to changing times and audience expectations. This adaptability has likely taught him the importance of embracing new opportunities, reinventing oneself, and staying relevant in a dynamic entertainment industry.

These lessons and personal growth experiences have likely shaped Paul O'Grady into the resilient, compassionate, and multifaceted individual he is today. His journey as an entertainer, philanthropist, and advocate has provided him with valuable insights that he can share with others, inspiring them to embrace their true selves, overcome challenges, and make a positive impact on the world.

CHAPTER NINE

9. Legacy and Influence

Paul O'Grady's legacy and influence are far-reaching and have left an indelible mark on the entertainment industry and beyond. Here are some key aspects of his legacy and the influence he has had:

1. Comedy and Entertainment: O'Grady's contributions to comedy and entertainment have had a lasting impact. His creation of the iconic character Lily Savage revolutionized the drag queen persona in the UK and brought it into the mainstream. His sharp wit, comedic timing, and ability to connect with audiences have inspired aspiring comedians and entertainers.

2. LGBTQ+ Representation: O'Grady's openness about his sexuality and his unapologetic portrayal of the flamboyant Lily Savage have helped break down barriers and promote LGBTQ+ visibility and acceptance. He has been a role model for many individuals within the LGBTQ+ community, showing them that it is possible to be true to oneself and achieve success.

3. Philanthropy and Advocacy: O'Grady's commitment to philanthropy and advocacy has had a significant impact on various causes. His work in supporting animal welfare, HIV/AIDS charities, children's charities, and LGBTQ+ rights has raised awareness and made a difference in the lives of many. His efforts have inspired others to get involved and contribute to charitable causes.

4. Television and Media Influence: As a television host and personality, O'Grady has shaped the landscape of British television. His talk show, "The Paul O'Grady Show," became a staple in daytime TV, attracting a loyal fan base. His engaging and relatable style of hosting has influenced other presenters and helped define the genre.

5. Cultural Icon: O'Grady's unique personality, infectious laughter, and memorable catchphrases have made him a cultural icon. He has become a recognizable figure in British popular culture, symbolizing humor, resilience, and authenticity. His impact on the entertainment industry has been acknowledged through various awards and accolades.

6. Literary Contributions: O'Grady's books, including his autobiographical works and children's books, have touched the lives of readers and left a lasting impression. His candid storytelling, humor, and insights into his own experiences have resonated with a wide audience and influenced aspiring writers.

7. Inspiration and Empowerment: O'Grady's journey, marked by overcoming personal challenges and embracing his true self, has inspired many individuals. His story serves as a reminder that with determination, resilience, and authenticity, one can overcome adversity and achieve success.

8. Enduring Popularity: O'Grady's popularity has stood the test of time. He continues to engage audiences through his television appearances, charitable work, and public persona. His enduring popularity reflects his ability to connect with people on a genuine and relatable level.

Paul O'Grady's legacy and influence extend beyond the entertainment industry. Through his humor, philanthropy, and advocacy, he has left an impact on society, inspiring others to be true to themselves, contribute to charitable causes, and promote inclusivity and acceptance. His influence will continue to resonate with generations to come.

9.1 Paul O'Grady's lasting impact on the Entertainment Industry

Paul O'Grady has made a lasting impact on the entertainment industry through his unique talents, groundbreaking contributions, and charismatic persona. Here are some of the ways in which he has influenced and shaped the entertainment landscape:

1. Redefining Drag Performance: With the creation of his drag queen persona, Lily Savage, O'Grady revolutionized the art of drag performance in the UK. Lily Savage became an iconic character known for her larger-than-life personality, sharp wit, and glamorous style. O'Grady's portrayal of Lily Savage challenged stereotypes and brought drag into the mainstream, paving the way for other drag performers and increasing the visibility and acceptance of the art form.

2. Blending Comedy and Candidness: O'Grady's comedic style, marked by his quick wit and candid storytelling, has captivated audiences for decades. His ability to blend humor with personal anecdotes and social commentary has set him apart as a comedian and entertainer. O'Grady's approach has influenced comedic performers by demonstrating the power of authenticity, relatability, and the ability to connect with audiences on a deeper level.

3. Versatility as a Television Host: O'Grady's success as a television host has showcased his versatility and adaptability. From hosting his own talk show to presenting game shows, documentaries, and travel programs, he has proven his ability to engage viewers across a variety of formats. His warm and affable demeanor, coupled with his natural rapport with guests, has set a standard for hosting excellence and inspired other presenters in the industry.

4. Philanthropy and Charitable Contributions: O'Grady's commitment to philanthropy and charitable causes has had a significant impact on the entertainment industry and beyond. His dedication to animal welfare, HIV/AIDS charities, children's charities, and LGBTQ+ rights has raised

awareness and provided support to numerous organizations. By using his platform to advocate for important causes, O'Grady has encouraged other entertainers to use their influence for positive change.

5. Literary Contributions: O'Grady's literary works, including his autobiographical books and children's literature, have added another dimension to his creative repertoire. His storytelling abilities and candid writing style have resonated with readers, allowing them to connect with his experiences and perspectives. O'Grady's success as an author has inspired other entertainers to explore writing as a means of self-expression and storytelling.

6. Enduring Popularity and Cultural Icon Status: O'Grady's enduring popularity and status as a cultural icon are testaments to his lasting impact on the entertainment industry. His infectious laughter, memorable catchphrases, and relatable personality have endeared him to audiences across generations. O'Grady's influence is evident in the continued affection and recognition he receives from fans, as well as the numerous awards and accolades he has received throughout his career.

Paul O'Grady's lasting impact on the entertainment industry is characterized by his ability to challenge norms, connect with audiences, and use his platform to make a positive difference. His contributions have left an indelible mark on the art of drag performance, comedy, television hosting, philanthropy, and literature. As an influential figure, O'Grady has shaped the industry and inspired countless individuals with his talent, authenticity, and dedication to making a meaningful impact through entertainment.

9.2 Influence on future generations of Performers

Paul O'Grady's influence on future generations of performers is significant and far-reaching. His contributions to the entertainment industry have inspired and paved the way for aspiring artists, comedians, and drag performers. Here's how O'Grady has influenced the next generation:

1. Authenticity and Self-Expression: O'Grady's unwavering commitment to authenticity and self-expression has empowered future performers to embrace their true selves. By fearlessly embodying his drag queen persona, Lily Savage, O'Grady has shown that being true to oneself is not only liberating but also inspiring to others. This has encouraged aspiring artists to explore and express their own unique identities and talents without fear of judgment or prejudice.

2. Diversity and Inclusion: O'Grady's portrayal of Lily Savage and his open discussions about his own sexuality have contributed to the acceptance and normalization of diverse identities within the entertainment industry. His inclusive approach has opened doors for performers from all walks of life, fostering an environment where diversity is celebrated and embraced. This has paved the way for future generations of performers to express their authentic selves and challenge societal norms.

3. Blending Comedy and Social Commentary: O'Grady's ability to infuse comedy with social commentary has inspired aspiring performers to use their art as a platform for meaningful messages. His wit and candidness have shown the power of humor in addressing social issues and sparking conversations. This influence can be seen in the rise of comedians who tackle important topics and use comedy as a tool for social change.

4. Philanthropy and Giving Back: O'Grady's dedication to philanthropy and charitable causes has set an example for future performers to use their influence and success to make a positive impact. His involvement in various charitable endeavors, particularly in the areas of animal welfare, HIV/AIDS charities, and LGBTQ+ rights, has inspired aspiring artists to align their careers with causes they are passionate about and actively contribute to society.

5. Versatility and Adaptability: O'Grady's ability to excel in different formats, from stand-up comedy to television hosting and writing, has shown aspiring performers the importance of versatility and adaptability. His success across various mediums demonstrates that being multi-talented and open to exploring different creative avenues can lead to a fulfilling and enduring career.

6. Resilience and Perseverance: O'Grady's personal and professional challenges, including the loss of his partner and health issues, have showcased his resilience and determination. His ability to overcome obstacles and continue pursuing his passions has inspired future performers to persevere in the face of adversity and never give up on their dreams.

7. Mentorship and Support: O'Grady's willingness to share his experiences and offer guidance to emerging performers has provided invaluable mentorship and support. Through his mentorship, he has helped shape and nurture the talents of aspiring artists, ensuring that the next generation is equipped with the necessary skills and knowledge to succeed in the industry.

Overall, Paul O'Grady's influence on future generations of performers is profound. His impact can be seen in the growing acceptance of diverse identities, the blending of comedy and social commentary, and the dedication to philanthropy and giving back. Aspiring artists look to O'Grady as a role model, drawing inspiration from his authenticity, resilience, and commitment to making a difference through entertainment.

9.3 Reflections on his contributions and cultural significance

Paul O'Grady's contributions to the entertainment industry and his cultural significance cannot be overstated. His talent, authenticity, and dedication have left an indelible mark on the hearts and minds of audiences worldwide. Here are some reflections on his contributions and cultural significance:

1. Pioneering Drag Performance: O'Grady's creation of the iconic character Lily Savage revolutionized drag performance in the UK and beyond. He broke barriers by bringing drag into the mainstream and challenging stereotypes associated with the art form. O'Grady's influence paved the way for a new generation of drag performers and expanded the possibilities of self-expression and gender exploration in entertainment.

2. Comedy and Social Commentary: O'Grady's comedic genius, characterized by his sharp wit and astute observations, has entertained and enlightened audiences for decades. He has used humor as a tool to address social issues, spark conversations, and challenge societal norms. O'Grady's ability to seamlessly blend comedy with social commentary has made him a cultural icon and an influential figure in the world of comedy.

3. LGBTQ+ Visibility and Acceptance: As an openly gay man, O'Grady has been a trailblazer in promoting LGBTQ+ visibility and acceptance. His openness about his sexuality and his portrayal of the flamboyant Lily Savage has helped break down barriers and increase understanding and tolerance. O'Grady's influence has been particularly impactful in inspiring LGBTQ+ individuals to embrace their identities and pursue their dreams without fear.

4. Philanthropic Impact: O'Grady's dedication to philanthropy and charitable causes has made a significant difference in the lives of many. His support for animal welfare, HIV/AIDS charities, children's

charities, and LGBTQ+ rights has raised awareness and provided crucial support to organizations in need. O'Grady's philanthropic efforts have inspired others to use their platforms for the betterment of society, creating a ripple effect of positive change.

5. Cultural Icon and National Treasure: O'Grady's status as a cultural icon and national treasure in the UK is a testament to his enduring popularity and cultural significance. His infectious laughter, memorable catchphrases, and relatable personality have endeared him to generations of fans. O'Grady's influence extends beyond his entertainment career, as he has become a symbol of resilience, authenticity, and compassion.

6. Inspiring Future Generations: Perhaps one of O'Grady's greatest contributions is the inspiration he has provided to future generations of performers and individuals. His journey, marked by personal triumphs and challenges, serves as a reminder that authenticity, perseverance, and compassion can lead to success and make a positive impact. O'Grady's legacy will continue to inspire and empower individuals to embrace their true selves and create change in their communities.

Paul O'Grady's contributions and cultural significance are immense. His pioneering work in drag performance, his comedic brilliance, and his advocacy for important causes have shaped the entertainment industry and left a lasting impact on society. O'Grady's influence will continue to resonate for years to come, as his legacy inspires future generations to be true to themselves, challenge norms, and use their platforms for the greater good.

CHAPTER TEN

10. Conclusion

In conclusion, the life of Paul O'Grady is a remarkable journey filled with triumphs, challenges, and a profound impact on the entertainment industry and society as a whole. From his humble beginnings to becoming a cultural icon, O'Grady has exemplified the power of talent, authenticity, and resilience.

Through the creation of his iconic drag queen persona, Lily Savage, O'Grady shattered stereotypes and brought drag performance into the mainstream. His ability to blend comedy with social commentary, coupled with his candidness and wit, has captivated audiences and inspired future generations of performers.

O'Grady's philanthropic efforts and advocacy work have made a tangible difference in the lives of many. His dedication to causes such as animal welfare, HIV/AIDS charities, and LGBTQ+ rights has raised awareness and provided support to numerous organizations. His legacy extends beyond entertainment, as he has become a symbol of compassion and generosity.

Throughout his career, O'Grady has overcome personal and professional challenges with resilience and perseverance. His ability to balance fame and personal life serves as a testament to his character and values. He has demonstrated the importance of staying true to oneself and using success to make a positive impact on the world.

Paul O'Grady's contributions and cultural significance will continue to resonate for years to come. His influence on drag performance, comedy, philanthropy, and advocacy will inspire future generations of performers and individuals to embrace their true selves, challenge societal norms, and use their platforms for the greater good.

"The Life of Paul O'Grady" is a story of triumph, compassion, and the power of authenticity. It is a celebration of a remarkable individual who has left an indelible mark on the entertainment industry and society, reminding us of the transformative power of laughter, compassion, and the pursuit of one's true passions.

10.1 Final thoughts on Paul O'Grady's remarkable life journey

Paul O'Grady's life journey is a testament to the transformative power of talent, authenticity, and perseverance. From his modest upbringing to becoming a beloved figure in the entertainment industry, O'Grady's story is filled with remarkable achievements, personal growth, and a deep commitment to making a positive impact on the world.

Throughout his career, O'Grady has challenged stereotypes, pushed boundaries, and inspired others to embrace their true selves. His creation of the iconic drag queen persona, Lily Savage, opened doors for drag performers and expanded the possibilities of self-expression. O'Grady's comedic brilliance and ability to blend humor with social commentary have left an indelible mark on the comedy landscape, encouraging future generations to use their voices to address important issues.

Beyond entertainment, O'Grady's philanthropic efforts and advocacy work have made a tangible difference in the lives of countless individuals and causes. His dedication to animal welfare, HIV/AIDS charities, children's charities, and LGBTQ+ rights has raised awareness and provided vital support. O'Grady's contributions go beyond financial assistance; his genuine compassion and willingness to use his platform for positive change have inspired others to do the same.

Despite facing personal and professional challenges, O'Grady has demonstrated unwavering resilience and an unwavering commitment to his values. His ability to balance fame and personal life is a testament to his character and priorities. O'Grady's authenticity, humility, and down-to-earth nature have endeared him to fans across generations, making him a beloved and relatable figure.

Paul O'Grady's life journey serves as a beacon of hope and inspiration for individuals striving to pursue their passions, overcome obstacles, and make a meaningful impact. His story reminds us of the power of staying true to oneself, embracing diversity, and using one's platform to uplift others. O'Grady's remarkable journey will continue to resonate with audiences and leave a lasting legacy for years to come.

"The Life of Paul O'Grady" is a celebration of a remarkable individual who has enriched the world with his talent, kindness, and unwavering spirit. It is a story that reminds us of the transformative power of authenticity, resilience, and compassion, inspiring us to embrace our own unique paths and strive to make a positive difference in the world.

Paul O'Grady was such a loving and peaceful man, he passed on as a fulfilled man at the age of 67 after suffering a cardiac arrhythmia. I hope the knowledge of his life and time will help us live a better and fulfilling life as Paul.

10.2 The enduring legacy of his work

The enduring legacy of Paul O'Grady's work is a testament to his immense talent, cultural impact, and unwavering commitment to authenticity and philanthropy. His contributions to the entertainment industry and society as a whole continue to resonate long after his performances and appearances.

One aspect of O'Grady's legacy is his influence on the world of drag performance. By creating the iconic character Lily Savage, he not only popularized drag in the mainstream but also challenged societal norms and paved the way for a more inclusive and diverse entertainment landscape. His fearless portrayal of Lily Savage inspired a new generation of drag performers to embrace their identities, express themselves authentically, and find success in the industry.

O'Grady's comedic brilliance and ability to seamlessly blend humor with social commentary have also left an indelible mark. His witty observations, sharp one-liners, and candid discussions about social issues have entertained audiences while provoking thought and sparking important conversations. O'Grady's comedic legacy continues to inspire comedians and performers to use their platforms for both laughter and social change.

Furthermore, O'Grady's philanthropic endeavors and advocacy work have had a lasting impact on various causes. His involvement in animal welfare, HIV/AIDS charities, children's charities, and LGBTQ+ rights has raised awareness, generated support, and positively impacted countless lives. O'Grady's dedication to giving back and using his influence for the greater good serves as an enduring example for others in the entertainment industry and beyond.

Moreover, O'Grady's personal journey of resilience, perseverance, and personal growth continues to inspire individuals facing their own challenges. His ability to overcome adversity, maintain authenticity, and find strength in difficult times resonates with people from all walks of life. O'Grady's story serves as a reminder that one's journey is not defined solely by success, but by the lessons learned, personal growth, and the impact made along the way.

In conclusion, Paul O'Grady's enduring legacy lies in his trailblazing contributions to drag performance, his comedic brilliance and social commentary, his philanthropic efforts, and his personal journey of resilience and authenticity. His work continues to inspire and entertain audiences, while his dedication to making a positive impact on society leaves a lasting impression. Paul O'Grady's legacy will be remembered and celebrated for generations to come.

Printed in Great Britain
by Amazon